ENGLISH TEATIME TREATS 3

THE BEST RECIPES FOR TARTS, PIES, AND MINI-PUDS MADE SIMPLE

SANDRA HAWKINS

Copyright © 2022 by Sandra Hawkins

All rights reserved. No part of this book may be reproduced in any form or by any electronic or mechanical means, including information storage and retrieval systems, without written permission from the author, except for the use of brief quotations in a book review.

First edition

Published by Great British Book Publishing, London

ISBN: 978-0-9957623-7-4
ISBN: 978-0-9957623-8-1

DEDICATION

To Simon and our children, Poppy, Monty and Barty

TABLE OF CONTENTS

Introduction — 1

Tarts and Pies

1. Treacle Tart — 7
2. Gypsy Tart — 11
3. Chocolate Tarts — 15
4. Cornflake Tart — 19
5. Fruit and Custard Tarts — 23
6. Mince Pies — 27
7. Lemon Meringue Pie — 31
8. Custard Slices — 35
9. Butterscotch Tart — 39
10. Lemon Tart — 43
11. Baked Custard Tart — 47
12. Honey and Walnut Tarts — 51
13. Banoffee Pies — 55
14. Chocolate and Pear Tart — 59
15. Jam Tarts and Lemon Curd Tarts — 63

Savory Tarts

16. Sausage Rolls — 69

17. Mini Quiches — 73

18. Cheese and Onion Square Tarts — 77

Mini-Puds

19. Mini-Knickerbocker Glory — 83

20. Chocolate Mousse — 87

21. Junket — 91

22. Mini-Fruit Cheesecakes — 95

23. Syllabub — 99

24. Eton Mess — 103

25. Lemon Posset and Shortbread Buttons — 107

26. Flummery — 111

27. Summer Puddings — 115

28. Fools — 119

29. Trifle — 123

30. Apple Snow — 127

Appendix – Pastry Tips — 131

Acknowledgements — 139

About the Author — 140

INVITATION

You are cordially invited to become an English Teatime Treater!

Sign up at the website below and you'll receive a FREE bonus recipe!

Check out the website for up-to-date promotions, competitions, the release date of future books, and all the latest news!

ett3.englishteatimetreats.com

INTRODUCTION

"Cooking and baking is both physical and mental therapy."

Mary Berry

"I love tarts and pies, but making pastry is fiddly and time-consuming."

"I like the idea of a homemade tart or dessert without all the fake colors and preservatives, but I just don't have the time or the energy for all the clearing up!"

"I know I'm a little bit stuck on making or buying the same desserts and would love a change, but I don't want to put in the effort and be disappointed."

I understand all these feelings. Life is full and pressured. All these recipes are quick and simple and need very little cleaning up afterward. You don't even have to make your own pastry for any of these recipes. You can buy ready-rolled pastry or even pre-baked pastry shells and just add the filling! Hey presto, a delicious tart, pie, or mini-pud (or mini-dessert) with very little effort and even less cleaning up!

Set out for you are the best recipes for these delicious little treats from the history of England. I can guarantee that you will be delighted with all these recipes and want to make them again and again.

Some recipes don't even involve turning on the oven! You can just buy the pastry case and fill it or whip up the ingredients. What could be more straightforward? And as I said in *English Teatime Treats 2: The Best Recipes From Around England Made Simple,* what great chef doesn't have a sous-chef to help with the preparation?

Not only are the recipes the best, but I have added stories of ingredients and recipes to intrigue and hopefully delight you. Maybe, like me, knowing something about the ingredients we take for granted and the stories that give birth to the recipes from ancient and more modern times will enhance your enjoyment of the treats.

I find it very grounding and fascinating that our ancestors ate similar things to us. These recipes all have some fun facts which draw on the stories of the past and pass on the golden thread of taste sensations to us today. You may feel this is rather a romantic, aromatic idea, but who hasn't smelt or tasted something and been transported back to an earlier memory?

What if you could simply whip up a celebration tart, pie, or mini-pud and invite others to enjoy it with you? Kids off the computer, friends relaxing and chatting, grandparents feeling loved. There is something almost mystical about sharing food together, particularly when you have made it yourself - and it's sweet!

Being in community with others is part of being human, and we are always told that connectivity is essential to our mental well-being. How can we connect more with people around us, our family and friends?

Enter the tart, pie, or mini-pud!

These recipes provide an opportunity to reconnect with others over something you have made for them. Invite a few friends over and enjoy the sweetness of friendship and tart. Reconnect with family over a teatime treat. It can be a bridge-builder or a fun celebration.

Time and time again, I have been so surprised at how appreciative people are when you create something for them. I have learned not to underestimate the value of a beautiful tart, pie, or mini-pud set in the middle of the table surrounded by expectant and happy onlookers.

Don't delay; make a tart today!

TARTS, PIES AND MINI-PUDS

Just so you know what I mean by tarts, pies, and mini-puds, I thought it might be helpful to define these words.

A tart is an open pastry case containing a sweet or savory filling.

A pie has a pastry lid as well as a pastry base. A flan and a quiche are usually open-topped, though a quiche is generally savory with an egg-based filling.

A mini-pud is a smaller version of an English pudding. In the U.S., pudding is a specific blancmange affair that often comes as a packet mix. Not so in England. Puddings in England come in all shapes and sizes and may be thought of more like a dessert that is served as the sweet course at the end of a meal.

Though the recipes for mini-puds can be used as desserts, I have crafted them to be added to your teatime table. They can all be eaten from their little pots, just with a teaspoon accompanied by a cup of tea!

DELICIOUS AND HISTORIC PASTRY

Some form of pastry has been used since antiquity. In the cradles of civilization, olive oil was used to bind the flour together to form a pastry. Pastry evolved in the Tudor period and incorporated fats and eggs, and began to be eaten with their contents. Tudor pies gained greater status and were elaborately decorated. So when you eat the pastry recipes, consider our ancestors and their stories!

I have drawn on the history of food eaten in England over the centuries to bring you the best teatime treat recipes. Because food and its history are such a passion of mine, I have provided some fun facts for each recipe for your enjoyment. The historical tidbits may be about the ingredients or even when the recipe was first made.

The recipes included are mainly sweet tarts, pies, and mini-puds, though there are a few savory recipes that I couldn't resist including because they are too delicious to miss!

TEA AT THE RITZ

There is, of course, never a wrong time of day to enjoy a tart, pie, or mini-pud. A slice of Treacle Tart can be enjoyed with morning coffee or a little sausage roll with lunch, but best of all is the teatime moment! The buttery pastry of a custard slice combined with the feathered icing, all melded together with a nice cup of tea - heaven!

I experienced a delicious tea at the Ritz Hotel, London recently to celebrate my birthday. Delightfully nestled on top of the teatime treats stand was the lemon tart!

FINALLY

Treat yourself and your family and friends to some of these recipes today. Join together and have some fun discovering the background of some of the best-loved English teatime tarts, pies, and mini-puds!

Let us start with the Treacle Tart - made with simple ingredients to give a wonderful result.

TARTS AND PIES

1. TREACLE TART

INTRODUCTION

The Treacle Tart is a delicious English pudding. It is very sweet, but the addition of lemon cuts through the sweetness. Substituting the lemon for an orange juice and zest and adding 2 teaspoons of ginger makes a wonderful variation.

FUN FACTS

Treacle is made from syrup after the sugar has been refined. The light color of golden syrup is pale gold. The darker-colored treacle is blacker with a slightly bitter flavor and is called molasses in other countries.

Treacle was once thought to have healing properties and was used by herbalists and apothecaries to treat snake and other poisonous animal bites. The name "treacle" comes from the ancient Greek *"theriaca antidotos,"* meaning "antidote for the bite of wild beasts."

The golden syrup used in this recipe was invented by the Eastick brothers in 1883 and marketed in 1885 by Abram Lyle & Sons (now Tate & Lyle). Mr. Lyle had strong Christian beliefs and wanted to design something to reflect that. He was reminded of the prophet Samson's riddle in the Bible, Judges 14, which says:

> *"out of the eater came something to eat;*
>
> *out of the strong came forth sweetness".*

One day Samson, who was mightily strong, killed a young lion who was attacking him. When he saw the carcass later, a swarm of bees had made it their home and produced a large quantity of honey. So the answer to his riddle was a lion filled with honey from bees.

Mr. Lyle designed his tin to include a picture of Samson's lion and bees and the words "out of the strong comes something sweet." Where bees produce honey from the carcass, so flows sweet syrup from the tin. I like to think that is a good reason to indulge now and then.

It was considered so delicious and energy-giving that Captain Scott took some on his Antarctic expedition in 1910.

In 2007 the Guinness World Records confirmed it is the oldest, largely unchanged packaging of a brand. So today, you can still see Samson's lion and part of his riddle on the tins.

This is my Uncle Nigel's favorite type of tart.

INGREDIENTS

Serves 8, 9-inch (23cm) large tart

Makes 12, 3¼-inch (8cm) individual tarts

- 13.2oz. (375g) shortcrust pastry to line a 9-inch (23cm) removable bottom cake pan or a pre-baked pastry case, or 12 pre-baked individual pastry cases
- 4½ cups (175g) freshly-made breadcrumbs (dried or frozen are a disaster)
- 2¼ cups (750g) golden syrup or corn syrup
- Zest and juice of 1 lemon
- 2 eggs

METHOD

For the pastry case:

1. Preheat the oven to 400°F (200°C) and place in a baking sheet to heat.
2. Line the cake pan with pastry and bake blind. (See Appendix - Pastry Tips for how to do this.) Reserve about 4oz. or 100g of pastry to make the lattice top.
3. Or use a pre-baked pastry case, either a whole case or small individual ones, and leave out the lattice top. It will still look great!

For the filling:

1. Warm the syrup in a pan, and when melted, add the remaining ingredients and mix thoroughly.
2. Spread over the cooked pastry case and smooth to level.
3. Roll out the reserved pastry and cut it into strips.
4. Lay these over the top of the tart to form a lattice pattern.
5. Place the tart on the preheated tray in the oven and bake for 35 minutes until golden brown.
6. For small tarts, use pre-baked small pastry cases and fill them with the treacle filling. Bake for 15-20 minutes until golden brown.
7. Serve with cream or ice cream as a dessert, or alone with tea.

A slice of treacle tart or an individual one is delicious served cold at teatime.

2. GYPSY TART

INTRODUCTION

So the story goes, a housewife saw some children from a traveling community playing outside. She thought they looked hungry. To feed them, she used her cupboard ingredients to create this tart for them.

Though the word "Gypsy" is considered racist now, it is still associated with this tart when served up in the County of Kent. Perhaps it would be better re-named Roma Tart? I'll leave that up to you.

Made with evaporated milk and dark brown sugar whipped together and poured onto a shortcrust pastry base, this tart is deliciously light and sweet.

FUN FACTS

The invention of evaporated milk used in this recipe has an interesting origin.

Cows used to be transported on ships to provide fresh milk for the passengers and crew. In 1840 when Cunard sailed across the Atlantic, a cow was brought on board to provide fresh milk. Its milk was enjoyed throughout the voyage and sadly for the cow, so was its steak on the last day!

In 1852, on a voyage across the Atlantic, the sea was so rough that the seasick cows on board could not be milked. This made Gail Borden, a young dairy farmer on board, wonder how milk could be preserved so that it wouldn't spoil.

Once home, he began experimenting with removing some of the water in an airtight pan to preserve the milk. He eventually came up with a product that didn't spoil; evaporated milk. This has been enjoyed ever since.

INGREDIENTS

Serves 8, 9-inch (23cm) large tart

Makes 12, 3¼-inch (8cm) individual tarts

- 13.2oz. (375g) shortcrust pastry to line a 9-inch (23 cm) removable bottom cake pan or a pre-baked pastry case, or 12 pre-baked individual pastry cases
- 12 fl oz. (410g or 1 tin) evaporated milk
- 1¼ cups (300g) dark brown sugar

METHOD

1. Preheat the oven to 400°F (200°C) and place in a baking sheet to heat.
2. Line the cake pan with pastry and bake blind. (See Appendix - Pastry Tips for how to do this.) Or use a pre-baked pastry case or individual pre-baked pastry cases.
3. Using a food mixer, whisk the sugar and milk on high speed for 10-15 minutes. It should be billowing and light coffee color. It seems like a long time - but it's worth it.
4. Pour into your pastry case and place on the preheated baking sheet, and put into the oven.
5. Bake for about 20 minutes until the tart has risen and is just about set. Be careful not to overcook.
6. When it comes out, it will flatten a little, which is what you should expect.
7. If making the individual tarts, reduce the baking time to 10 minutes.

Leave to cool and serve with cream or ice cream or as it is with a cup of tea.

3. CHOCOLATE TARTS

INTRODUCTION

These gleaming chocolate ganache tarts are a dream to make and eat! The thick, really chocolate center contrasts with the buttery crisp pastry beautifully.

FUN FACTS

The amazing thing about chocolate is that it melts in the mouth. It's because the cocoa fat becomes a liquid at just below body temperature. How wonderful is that? That's why I find chunks of chocolate in ice cream not very satisfying because it is too cold to melt, and you end up crunching it and not getting that wonderful bliss of the chocolate melt in the mouth. But you may disagree!

The history of chocolate goes back to at least the Mayans in the first century AD when it was drunk as a frothy drink. We know that the froth was created by pouring it from vessel to vessel from painted vases showing the action. It was sometimes flavored with chili or vanilla. The Aztecs considered it a drink for warriors and the elite. They added honey to sweeten it, and the Spanish added sugar.

Chocolate was first sold in London in about 1657 AD. In the 1660s, Samuel Pepys, of the diaries' fame, mentions a morning drink of chocolate.

Chocolate in the form we know and love today was created after the industrial revolution. In 1847, the English Chocolatier J.S. Fry made chocolate moldable. He mixed the ingredients of cocoa powder and sugar with melted cocoa butter. It became the first portable chocolate snack.

Milk powder was added by the Swiss chocolatier Daniel Peters in 1876, but it was still rather hard and crunchy. It didn't become creamy and smooth until about 1879 when Rudolf Lindt invented a way for it to be mixed and aerated to become melt-in-the-mouth.

Enjoy these melt-in-the-mouth tarts.

INGREDIENTS

Serves 8, 9-inch (23cm) large tart

Makes 12, 3¼-inch (8cm) individual tarts

- 13.2oz. (375g) shortcrust pastry to line a 9-inch (23 cm) removable bottom cake pan or a pre-baked pastry case, or 12 pre-baked individual pastry cases
- 2 cups (340g) dark chocolate, chopped into small pieces
- 1 cup (240ml) heavy (double) cream

METHOD

1. Line the cake pan with pastry and bake blind. (See Appendix - Pastry Tips for how to do this.) Or use a pre-baked pastry case or individual pre-baked pastry cases.
2. Warm the cream in a pan until tiny bubbles appear around the edge - but don't let it boil.
3. Turn off the heat and add the chocolate to the cream. Leave for a few minutes for the chocolate to begin to melt, and then stir and combine the two ingredients. It will thicken nicely and turn into ganache.
4. Add the ganache to the pastry case or cases and smooth over.
5. Leave to become firm in the fridge.

Cut into slices or serve individual tarts at teatime and enjoy!

4. CORNFLAKE TART

INTRODUCTION

At school, I used to sit in a drafty prefabricated lunch hall chewing stringy beans, so looking forward to the pudding course: Cornflake Tart being one of the best!

It is a shortcrust pastry base with the crunchy sweetness of the cornflake filling and the strawberry jelly or jam layer. It can be served warm with custard as a dessert or on its own at teatime. This is bliss!

FUN FACTS

Cornflakes have been around since 1894 - invented by William Kellogg to feed the Sanatorium patients where his brother was the superintendent. Sadly, the brothers didn't seem to get on very well and battled over the patent for the flakes.

Interestingly, the brand Kellogg uses a cockerel or rooster in its marketing and always has done. It originated from a friend of the Kelloggs from Wales who commented that the Kellogg name was similar to *ceiliog*, the Welsh word for rooster. It's a strange way to choose a mascot for a brand!

INGREDIENTS

Serves 8, 9-inch (23cm) large tart

Makes 12, 3¼-inch (8cm) individual tarts

- 13.2oz. (375g) shortcrust pastry to line a 9-inch (23 cm) removable bottom cake pan or a pre-baked pastry case, or 12 pre-baked individual pastry cases
- ¼ cup or ½ stick (60g) butter
- 2 tablespoons superfine (caster) sugar
- ⅓ cup (110g) golden syrup or corn syrup
- 4 cups (100g) cornflakes
- 3 tablespoons strawberry jelly (jam)

METHOD

1. Preheat the oven to 400°F (200°C) and place in a baking sheet to heat.
2. Line the cake pan with pastry and bake blind. (See Appendix - Pastry Tips for how to do this.) Or use a pre-baked pastry case or individual pre-baked pastry cases.
3. Melt the butter in a pan and add the sugar and syrup.
4. Mix in the cornflakes.
5. Spread the jelly (jam) over the pastry base and smooth over the cornflake mixture.
6. Bake in the oven on the preheated tray for 5-8 minutes.
7. Leave to cool slightly before slicing into pieces.

Serve warm with custard as a dessert or alone with tea.

5. FRUIT AND CUSTARD TARTS

INTRODUCTION

These tarts have a shortcrust pastry base, filled with custard and topped with seasonal fruits. This recipe makes the custard on the hob, and when it is cool, the tarts are assembled.

Any fruit works well. I suggest whatever is seasonal or your favorites. If you are making individual tarts, you could decorate each one differently.

FUN FACTS

Food historians generally agree that custard in the form we recognize today dates back to the Middle Ages. It was either eaten by itself or as a filling for pies or tarts. Custard tarts were very popular in the Middle Ages. The word custard is derived from the French word *croustade*, meaning the crust of a tart which was usually filled with custard.

Traditionally, custard is made with cream and milk, eggs, and sugar. I have included the addition of cornstarch or cornflour, which helps thicken the custard or creme patisserie and stops it from curdling.

Medieval recipes generally included a pastry case filled with a sweetened mixture of cream, milk, or broth, with eggs, and sometimes spices. It was also considered to have health-giving properties.

Many custard recipes can be found in the 14th-century book *The Forme of Cury*, published in 1390 AD. A particular favorite of mine is the recipe for Eggs in Custard, where saffron is added, presumably for the color. Also, we are admonished to "let it not boil," which is still excellent advice for today.

INGREDIENTS

Serves 8, 9-inch (23 cm) large tart

Makes 12, 3¼-inch (8 cm) individual tarts

- 13.2oz. (375g) shortcrust pastry to line a 9-inch (23 cm) removable bottom cake pan or a pre-baked pastry case, or 12 pre-baked individual pastry cases
- Custard filling
- 2 cups (480ml) whole milk
- 1 teaspoon vanilla extract
- 6 tablespoons superfine (caster) sugar
- 2½ tablespoons (60g) cornstarch (cornflour)
- 3 egg yolks
- 1 egg
- 3 tablespoons (40g) butter

Fruit topping

- 350g strawberries
- 350g raspberries

METHOD

1. Line the cake pan with pastry and bake blind. (See Appendix - Pastry Tips for how to do this.) Or use a pre-baked pastry case or individual pre-baked pastry cases.
2. Heat the milk and vanilla extract together.

3. Whisk the sugar, egg yolks, whole egg, and cornstarch (cornflour) in a bowl.

4. Whisk into your egg mixture the heated milk and return the mixture to the pan.

5. Heat while whisking and when it has thickened, whisk in the butter a little at a time until it is all incorporated.

6. Transfer to a bowl, cover with cling film, and leave to cool.

7. When cool, spoon into the pastry cases and decorate artistically with the fresh summer fruit.

Leave in the fridge until you are ready to serve these little tarts.

6. MINCE PIES

INTRODUCTION

You can use shortcrust pastry, which is more traditional, but I have used puff pastry, giving a lighter result. But I must warn you; it makes them very moreish!

Homemade mincemeat has a much better flavor than store-bought varieties. But if you don't want to make it, you can add the zest of 2 oranges and a couple of tablespoons of brandy to your jar to enhance the flavor.

FUN FACTS

You may be wondering what the difference is between raisins, sultanas, and currants. Well, the similarity is that they all come from white grapes and are dried. The difference is the variety of grapes they come from and the way they are dried. Raisins darken when they dry, sultanas come from seedless white grapes which stay light, and currants are dried small white grapes which are less sweet and more tangy.

I love the way old recipes often were borne out of necessity rather than just invented for fun. Mincemeat pies are no exception to this. Mincemeat pies or minced meat pies originally came about as a good way of preserving meat. They provided a change from salting, curing, smoking, or drying. The mincemeat pies consisted of finely chopped meat mixed with fruit and suet, animal fat, and vinegar. Henry V served these pies at his coronation in 1413 AD.

By the mid-twentieth century, these pies no longer contained meat but still had suet or animal fat in them. I have used butter instead of suet in the following recipe because I think the flavor is so much better. Traditionally, mince pies were almost always prepared as small pies.

I have made a medieval recipe for minced meat pies using a layer of beef topped with pumpkin spice or mixed spice, brown sugar, raisins, sultanas, and currants. It was surprisingly delicious!

INGREDIENTS

Makes 24

Quick mincemeat

- 1 small Bramley apple or a large Granny Smith
- 1 cup (150g) currants
- 1 cup (150g) sultanas
- 1 cup (150g) raisins
- 1 cup (220g) dark brown sugar
- Zest 1 orange
- Zest 1 lemon
- 1½ teaspoon mixed (pumpkin) spice
- ¼ cup or ½ stick (60g) butter
- 1 tablespoon brandy (optional)

Mince pies

- 1 block (500g) ready-made puff pastry
- Mincemeat as above, or a jar of about 400g
- Powdered (icing) sugar to serve

METHOD

1. Preheat the oven to 400°F (200°C). Grease and flour your mince pie tins.
2. Make your quick mincemeat by mixing all the ingredients in a pan, except the brandy.

Warm this on the hob so the butter melts and covers the ingredients. It will only take a couple of minutes. Stir thoroughly and add the brandy. Set aside. The sugar will be melting, and all the buttery sweetness will coat the fruit.

3. Roll out the puff pastry on a lightly floured surface. Cut out 24 circles using a 3¼-inch or 8cm round pastry cutter. You should be able to get 24. You will need to gather it up and roll it out again, though. Try to keep the pastry's orientation the same when you gather it up to roll out again, so it is more like folding it back on itself. In this way, the layers of the puff pastry will be better preserved. Stamp out 24 little stars from the leftover pastry.

4. Use the circles to line the mince pie tins.

5. Add a spoonful of mincemeat into each one, press down slightly, and pop a star on top.

6. Place in the preheated oven for about 15 minutes.

7. Leave to cool and serve dusted with powdered (icing) sugar.

These are aromatic and melt in the mouth.

7. LEMON MERINGUE PIE

INTRODUCTION

With cream - what could be more delicious? This has a buttery pastry base, a tart lemon filling, and a billowy meringue top. It won't last long!

FUN FACTS

Recipes for fruit desserts covered with baked meringue were enjoyed in France from the beginning of the 18th century. A recipe for a custard flavored with lemon and covered with baked meringue, *crème meringuée*, was published in 1769 in English.

Meringue has an interesting history. In the 16th century, egg whites were beaten to make an uncooked dish called "snow," which mixed the egg whites with cream. This was the beginning of the meringue. But the cooking of the snow would not have resulted in a meringue as the addition of fat would have stopped the egg whites from taking on the stiff foam-like quality.

The cooking of beaten egg whites with sugar made its appearance in the 17th century and was called sugar puff.

The name meringue is a direct borrowing from the French word, "*meringue*." It is said that Marie Antoinette enjoyed these sugary delights.

There is a certain wonderful symmetry about this recipe. The idea of topping the lemony custard with meringue probably comes from the fact that there are leftover egg whites, and what better way to use them up than topping off a lemony tart?

I love recipes that don't leave you with leftover egg whites or yolks to use up or leave in the fridge until you don't feel too guilty about throwing them away! All yolks and whites are used in this recipe.

INGREDIENTS

Serves 8, 9-inch (23cm) large tart

Makes 12, 3¼-inch (8cm) individual tarts

- 13.2oz. (375g) shortcrust pastry to line 9 inch (23 cm) removable bottom cake pan or a pre-baked pastry case, or 12 pre-baked individual pastry cases
- ¼ cup (50g) superfine (caster) sugar
- 3 tablespoons cornstarch (cornflour)
- 1 cup (240ml) water
- Zest and juice of 2 lemons
- 3 egg yolks (save the whites for the meringue topping)
- ¼ cup or ½ stick (60g) butter

Meringue topping

- 3 egg whites
- 1 cup (200g) superfine (caster) sugar

METHOD

For the pastry base

1. Preheat the oven to 300°F (150°C) and place in a baking sheet to heat.
2. Line the cake pan with pastry and bake blind. (See Appendix - Pastry Tips for how to do this.) Or use a pre-baked pastry case or individual pre-baked pastry cases.

For the lemon filling

1. Mix the cornflour and enough of the water to form a paste.
2. Pour the rest of the water and the cornflour mixture into a pan with the lemon zest and whisk together until it thickens.
3. Remove from heat and whisk in the lemon juice and the butter.
4. Smooth over the pastry case.

For the meringue topping

1. Whisk the egg whites together until they form peaks.
2. Add the sugar a tablespoon at a time until it is all incorporated.
3. Spoon over the lemon filling.
4. Place on the preheated baking tray and bake for about 45 minutes until the meringue is a pale golden color.

If you are making individual lemon meringue pies, reduce the baking time to 20 minutes.

Leave to cool and serve with a dollop of cream and a cup of tea.

8. CUSTARD SLICES

INTRODUCTION

Wedged between puff pastry topped with icing, the custard is creamy, smooth, and delicious.

FUN FACTS

Alfred Bird invented custard powder in 1837. Alfred Bird's wife suffered from an egg allergy, so he created a custard that his wife could enjoy. Being a Chemist, he used his knowledge to create an alternative. To thicken the custard, he added cornstarch (cornflour) instead of eggs so his wife could join in the pudding fun! Rather romantic.

Alfred Bird's egg-free custard was his first major invention. One evening he served it to his guests instead of normal custard, and it was greeted with delight. That was when he realized his custard powder might have the potential for a wider audience. Bird's Custard company was born. It was extremely successful largely because there was no longer the worry of the custard curdling if boiled, and he was a skillful marketer.

I have topped the custard slices with feather icing. I think it is so pretty and is much easier than it looks! Give it a go. When I first made this as a child, I couldn't believe how impressive and easy it was. You just need a steady hand.

INGREDIENTS

Makes 12

For the pastry

- 1 sheet ready-rolled puff pastry

For the filling

- 2 cups (480ml) heavy (double) cream

- ¾ cup (150g) superfine (caster) sugar
- ½ cup (65g) custard powder
- 1 teaspoon vanilla extract
- ¾ cup (180ml) whole milk

For the frosting (icing)

- 1⅓ cups (180g) powdered sugar (icing)
- 2 tablespoons water
- 1 teaspoon cocoa powder for the feathering

METHOD

1. Preheat the oven to 400°F (200°C).
2. Unroll your puff pastry and cut it in half, and place both halves on a baking sheet.
3. Prick them all over with a fork so that they don't puff up too much.
4. Bake for 15 minutes until pale brown and remove from the oven. That's the end of the baking.
5. After about 2 minutes out of the oven, place a tea towel on top of the pastry halves and gently press down so that it is a little more flattened. Transfer to a cooling rack and then leave to cool completely.

Make the custard while the pastry is cooling:

1. In a large pan, mix the sugar and custard powder.
2. Add about a third of the cream to form a paste, and then add the rest of the cream, the milk and the vanilla extract.
3. Turn on the heat and gently stir with a whisk.

4. Keep the heat low as it easily catches on the bottom of the pan when it is thickening.

5. Once thickened (it may take about 10 minutes), transfer to a bowl, place some cling film or tin foil directly on the surface to avoid the custard forming a skin, and leave to cool.

Feather icing:

1. When the pastry has cooled, mix the powdered (icing) sugar with the water to form a thick icing.

2. Transfer a tablespoon to a small bowl and add a teaspoon of cocoa and a few drops of water so it's a thick runny consistency.

3. Smooth the white icing over one of the pastries.

4. Immediately using a teaspoon, drizzle the chocolate icing in straight lines over the white icing about 1cm apart from left to right. It doesn't matter if it's slightly wobbly because it won't be noticeable when the custard slices are cut up.

5. Next, take a cocktail stick or bamboo skewer and drag it across the chocolate lines from top to bottom, then bottom to top, to create the wonderful feathered effect.

6. Leave to set.

Assembling:

1. Put the plain sheet of pastry into a tray that it fits (my roasting tin fits the pastry perfectly in one half of it).

2. Spread the cold custard over the pastry. It will be nice and thick.

3. Cut the iced pastry into twelve equal pieces and refit them together on top of the custard. This means when you come to serve the slices; all the custard won't be squashed out as you cut down.

4. Leave in the fridge until you are ready to serve or for an hour to settle. When needed, cut down through the gaps in the iced pastry through the custard and the pastry base. Place on your serving platter.

It will keep for 3-4 days, but I can guarantee it will be gone before then!

9. BUTTERSCOTCH TART

INTRODUCTION

A sweet, smooth, butterscotch filling encased in buttery pastry. Once you have tried this tart which is so easy to make, I'm convinced it'll be a firm favorite. Unashamedly sweet, there is something wanton about this tart - but I suggest you just go with it!

FUN FACTS

If you have never tried this tart- you have missed a treat. As a schoolgirl, I can remember sitting in a drafty post-war prefabricated building eating over-cooked cold cabbage and feeling rather despondent with the day's lunch offering when pudding was brought out: Butterscotch Tart. Instantly my spirits lifted. The Butterscotch Tart with buttery pastry and sweet, creamy filling was utterly delicious and kept me going through double Maths in the afternoon.

There is some discussion about where the name came from. Butterscotch candies or sweets are a very crisp form of toffee containing butter and sometimes milk or cream. They are usually made by boiling brown sugar with butter and sometimes a little lemon juice. It may appear to be from Scotland due to scotch in the word, but I think it is most likely to have come from the adulteration of the word scotched or scorched butter, an original ingredient of the confectionery.

Butterscotch sweets or candies have been attributed to Doncaster in the North of England. In fact, in 1851, Queen Victoria was given a tin of these famous candies when she visited Doncaster.

This tart has a smooth butterscotch filling. It is best made the day before to give it plenty of time to chill overnight.

INGREDIENTS

Serves 8, 9-inch (23cm) large tart

Makes 12, 3¼-inch (8cm) individual tarts

- 13.2oz. (375g) shortcrust pastry to line a 9-inch (23 cm) removable bottom cake pan or a pre-baked pastry case, or 12 pre-baked individual pastry cases
- 1¼ cups or 2½ sticks (250g) butter
- 2¼ cups (500g) light brown sugar
- ⅔ cup (180ml) full-fat milk
- 2 tablespoons all-purpose (plain) flour

METHOD

1. Preheat the oven to 400°F (200°C) and place in a baking sheet to heat.
2. Line the cake pan with pastry and bake blind. (See Appendix - Pastry Tips for how to do this.) Or use a pre-baked pastry case or individual pre-baked pastry cases.
3. Melt the butter in a pan with the sugar and milk.
4. Whisk in the flour and heat until it thickens, then turn the heat down and cook gently for 2 minutes.
5. Pour into the pastry case or cases and chill overnight.
6. You can decorate as the mood takes you, but I love the gleam of the unadulterated butterscotch and the promise of its creamy, sweet texture.

If you wish, serve with ice cream or cream.

10. LEMON TART

INTRODUCTION

For teatime, I think a little lemon tart works best rather than a slice. The tartness of the lemon contrasted with the sweetness of the cream is one of my favorite combinations.

The Ritz Hotel in London serves lemon tart as part of their teatime offerings.

FUN FACTS

Lemons probably originated in India, in the Himalayas. Arab traders came from India with lemons to the Middle East and Africa. Crusaders in Medieval times found lemons growing in Palestine and brought them back to England.

Due to their high vitamin C content, lemons were essential for preventing scurvy on long sea voyages. The irony is that the sailors transporting lemons had the very cure for the disease that ailed them without even knowing. The British naval surgeon, James Lind, endorsed lemons as a cure in 1753, and by the end of the century, lemon juice was being given to sailors to cure scurvy.

Lemons came to the New World in 1493 AD when Columbus brought some lemon seeds over with him to Haiti. Within 20 years, there were abundant crops of good quality lemons. Lemons are now grown all over the world, though only in greenhouses in England.

INGREDIENTS

Serves 8, 9-inch (23cm) large tart

Makes 12, 3¼-inch (8cm) individual tarts

- 13.2oz. (375g) shortcrust pastry to line a 9-inch (23 cm) removable bottom cake pan or a pre-baked pastry case, or 12 pre-baked individual pastry cases.
- ¾ cup (150g) superfine (caster) sugar
- 5 eggs
- 5 lemons, zest, and just under 1 cup (225ml) juice
- ¾ cup (180ml) heavy (double) cream

METHOD

1. Preheat the oven to 350°F (180°C) and place in a baking sheet to heat.
2. Line the cake pan with pastry and bake blind. (See Appendix - Pastry Tips for how to do this.) Or use a pre-baked pastry case or individual pre-baked pastry cases.
3. Mix the sugar and eggs together.
4. Whisk in the lemon juice, zest, and cream.
5. Pour into the pre-baked pastry case or individual cases.
6. . Place on the preheated baking sheet and bake for 25 minutes for the large tart and 15 minutes for the small ones.
7. Dust with powdered sugar (icing) sugar before serving.

11. BAKED CUSTARD TART

INTRODUCTION

This uses a custard made from scratch with eggs and cream. There is a moment for using custard powder, but I think this recipe benefits from the egg custard. And it is traditionally made this way. As it sets in the oven, there is no need to be concerned about it curdling.

FUN FACTS

Medieval recipes existed that would still be recognizable as custard tarts today. In 1399 AD, the coronation banquet prepared for Henry IV included a type of custard tart. These tarts generally included either a shortcrust or a puff pastry case filled with a mixture of cream, milk, or broth, with eggs. Sugar or honey was used to sweeten the custard, and sometimes spices were added.

Traditionally, grated nutmeg is the spice of choice to top off these tarts, though you can use cinnamon if you prefer, which was more usual in France.

INGREDIENTS

Serves 8, 9-inch (23cm) large tart

Makes 12, 3¼-inch (8cm) individual tarts

- 13.2oz. (375g) shortcrust pastry to line 9 inch (23 cm) removable bottom cake pan or a pre-baked pastry case, or 12 pre-baked individual pastry cases
- 2 tablespoons (55g) superfine (caster) sugar
- 3 large eggs
- ½ teaspoon vanilla extract
- 1¾ cups (400ml) cream
- Grated nutmeg for the top

METHOD

1. Preheat the oven to 350°F (180°C) and place in a baking sheet to heat.
2. Line the cake pan with pastry and bake blind. (See Appendix - Pastry Tips for how to do this.) Or use a pre-baked pastry case or individual pre-baked pastry cases.
3. Whisk together the sugar, eggs, and the vanilla extract in a bowl.
4. Heat the cream in a pan.
5. Once hot, add the cream to the sugar and egg mixture and whisk together. It will thicken only a little at this stage as the cooking is done in the oven.
6. Remove the preheated baking sheet from the oven and place the pastry case on it.
7. Pour the custard mixture onto the pastry base and generously grate over some nutmeg.
8. Bake in the oven for 25-30 minutes until set but still slightly wobbly.
9. If making individual tarts, bake for 15 minutes.

Serve cold or warm.

12. HONEY AND WALNUT TARTS

INTRODUCTION

These are so easy to make and use brown sugar, which gives them a warm, rich flavor contrasting with the crunch and chew of the walnuts. They work very well as part of your teatime or as a mini-dessert. You can substitute raisins for walnuts if you prefer.

FUN FACTS

Walnuts were called Jupiter's royal acorn by the Romans. According to myth, when Jupiter walked the earth, he lived solely on the bounty of the walnut.

They came to England from Persia, where they were deemed so delicious they were reserved for royalty. The English were largely responsible for the early walnut trade recognizing their qualities and value.

We are interested in the culinary delights of walnuts, but I cannot resist sharing something of the Italian Renaissance when the moment arises. It is thought that artists including Leonardo da Vinci and Rembrandt used the husk of walnuts to make durable ink for writing and drawing. Delicious inside and useful outside.

INGREDIENTS

Makes 24

- 13.2oz. (375g) shortcrust pastry
- 1 cup (200g) walnut pieces (or raisins)
- 3 egg yolks
- 3 whole eggs
- 1½ (200g) cups light brown sugar
- 1 cup (340g) clear honey
- 2 tablespoons heavy (double) cream
- 1 tablespoon all-purpose (plain) flour

METHOD

1. Preheat the oven to 400°F (200°C). Grease and flour your little tart pans.
2. Unroll your ready-rolled pastry or roll it out on a lightly floured surface. Cut out 24 circles using a 3¼-inch or 8cm round pastry cutter. You should be able to get 24. You will need to gather it up and roll it out again, though.
3. Use the circles to line the tart pans. There is no need to bake blind.
4. Whisk together all the ingredients except the walnuts.
5. Mix in the walnuts. And spoon into the little pastry cases.
6. Bake in the oven for about 20 minutes until golden brown.

Leave to cool and serve.

13. BANOFFEE PIES

INTRODUCTION

Banoffee Pie is named after a portmanteau of banana and toffee making Banoffee. It was invented in 1971 by Nigel MacKensie at the Hungry Monk Restaurant in East Sussex, where it was an instant success. In 2019, it was named in the top 10 of English desserts according to Delicious Magazine.

FUN FACTS

The main ingredient, condensed milk, used to be called sweetened condensed milk. I imagine sweetened was deleted from its name because the manufacturers didn't want to draw attention to the fact that it has loads of added sugar. Anyway, it certainly is sweetened, but it's worth a little indulgence for this pie. One of my neighbors used to eat condensed milk straight from the tin - dear Don Piggot.

Moving to bananas, in England, the first recorded sale of bananas was in 1633. Thomas Johnson, a botanist, and merchant, displayed a bunch in his shop in Holborn, London, on April 10, 1633. The single stem of bananas came from the recently colonized island of Bermuda.

The banana did not become popular until the 19th century when the head gardener at Chatsworth House, Derbyshire, England, John Paxton, created a new variety. After spending several years developing his banana, in 1835, his variety won him a prize from the Royal Horticultural Society.

He named his winning variety the Cavendish. It is named after the family name of the owners of the Chatsworth Estate, the Duke and Duchess of Devonshire.

In 1835 his plant finally bore fruit. Most probably, the bananas you buy in England are descended from his Cavendish variety.

INGREDIENTS

For mini Banoffee Pies, use 2oz. pots

Makes about 20

- ½ cup or 1 stick (110g) butter, melted
- 15 Graham crackers or 15 digestive biscuits (225g) crushed

For the filling

- ⅓ cup (75g) butter
- ⅓ cup (75g) dark brown sugar
- 1 can 397g condensed milk
- 3 bananas
- ⅔ cup (160ml) heavy (double) cream or aerosol cream

METHOD

For the biscuit base:

1. Melt the butter and mix in the crushed Graham crackers or digestive biscuits.
2. Put 2 teaspoons of the crumb mixture into the bottom of your little pots and press down firmly.
3. Put them to one side to cool.

For the caramel:

1. Melt the butter and sugar in a pan.
2. Add the condensed milk and stir the mixture continuously until it comes to a boil for about a minute. It should be a golden caramel color and will have thickened up. Leave to cool a little.

To assemble:

1. While the caramel is cooling a little, chop up the bananas.

2. Put 2 teaspoonfuls of chopped bananas over the biscuit base in each pot.

3. Next, add about 2 teaspoons of caramel over the bananas. If you are using clear pots, you can see the attractive layers of biscuit, bananas, and then caramel.

4. Put it in the fridge to cool properly (it takes about an hour), as the cream will melt if the caramel is not cooled.

5. If you are using aerosol cream, leave the pots in the fridge until you are about to serve them, then add a squirt of cream and a little flower to decorate - I've used marigold petals.

6. If you are using whipped cream, whip the cream and place a heaped teaspoon on top, decorate, and put it back into the fridge until you are ready to serve.

The creamy sweetness of the caramel and bananas are so delicious set against the crunch of the biscuit base - I don't think one is enough!

14. CHOCOLATE AND PEAR TART

INTRODUCTION

Fruit paired with chocolate is not always a success, I feel. However, pear and chocolate do work. The grainy sweetness of the pear with the slightly bitter chocolate is a winner.

FUN FACTS

The Royal Horticultural Society held a Pear Conference in 1885 and an Apple and Pear Conference in 1888 at their gardens in Chiswick, London. The chairman of the Conference had created a new variety of mid-season dessert pear, which he exhibited. He won first prize for it, and it became known as the Conference Pear.

The famous Warden pear was raised in England by the Cistercian monks at the abbey in Bedfordshire. It became so important that many old recipes use the word Warden interchangeably with pear.

Pears do seem to lack the same allure as apples. I wonder if that's because it is difficult to time the ripening of the pear correctly - either rock-hard or over-ripe. This recipe is perfect for any pear that may not be perfectly ripe because it is cooked until it is softened to the point of deliciousness anyway.

INGREDIENTS

- 13.2 oz. (375g) shortcrust pastry
- ½ cup or 1 stick (110g) butter
- 1 cup (200g) superfine (caster) sugar
- 2 eggs
- ⅔ cup (100g) plain chocolate, melted
- 1 cup (100g) ground almonds
- 2 tablespoons plain flour
- 2 pears, peeled and sliced
- 1 tablespoon apricot jelly (jam)

METHOD

Makes 24

1. Preheat the oven to 400°F (200°C). Grease and flour your little pie pans.
2. Unroll your ready-rolled pastry or roll it out on a lightly floured surface. Cut out 24 circles using a 3¼-inch or 8cm round pastry cutter. You should be able to get 24. You will need to gather it up and roll it out again, though.
3. Use the circles to line the pie tins. There is no need to bake blind.
4. Melt the chocolate and leave it to cool.
5. Peel the pears, cut into quarters and remove the core. Slice up the quarters.
6. Cream together the butter and sugar until it is paler in color.
7. Add the eggs, ground almonds, flour, and melted chocolate and mix together.

8. Place a tablespoon of mixture into each pastry case.

9. Cut the pear slices so three fit nicely on top of each tart. Press the pear into the mixture.

10. Put the pans in the oven and bake for about 25 minutes.

11. Warm the apricot jelly (jam) in a saucepan with a tablespoon of water and dissolve the jelly (jam). Brush over the tarts when they come out of the oven and leave to cool.

Serve and enjoy.

15. JAM TARTS AND LEMON CURD TARTS

INTRODUCTION

If you ever have any leftover pastry, these are so simple and quick to whip up. I hate to waste anything, so you can easily make a few - though they will be munched very quickly. You may decide it is prudent to make a large batch.

FUN FACTS

Jams and curds have been used traditionally to preserve fruit during the winter months. The ancient Greeks used honey to preserve quinces. On the arrival of cane sugar to Europe in the 16th century, it was used to preserve fruit, hence the name preserves.

There is a lovely recipe from 1747 AD for raspberry jam which states it will keep for 2-3 years and will have the full flavor of raspberry.

Jane Austen's mother, Cassandra Austen, published a recipe for jam tarts, and she makes her pastry using half butter and half lard. She admonishes us not to "overfill or the jam will boil over and make a very sticky mess." Very good advice!

I have made three different flavored tarts as they look so colorful and pretty.

INGREDIENTS

Makes 24

- 13.2 oz. (375g) shortcrust pastry
- 1⅓ cup (275g) strawberry, blackcurrant jelly (jam), or lemon curd

METHOD

1. Preheat the oven to 400°F (200°C). Grease and flour your jam tart pans.

2. Unroll your ready-rolled pastry or roll it out on a lightly floured surface. Cut out 24 circles using a 3¼-inch or 8cm round pastry cutter. You should be able to get 24. You will need to gather it up and roll it out again, though.

3. Place these pastry circles in the holes.

4. Fill each pastry circle with one heaped teaspoon of jam or lemon curd. Don't overfill, as it will bubble up and make the tarts difficult to remove.

5. Bake in the preheated oven for 15 minutes until the jam begins to bubble and the pastry looks a pale golden color.

6. Leave to cool for 5 minutes in the pan before carefully removing to a cooling rack.

7. Leave to cool completely.

Eat cold with a cup of tea.

SAVORY TARTS

16. SAUSAGE ROLLS

INTRODUCTION

Greggs, the UK bakery giant, sells around 2.5 million sausage rolls per week in the UK, showing how much the English love the sausage roll. But these are even more delicious!

FUN FACTS

From a cuneiform tablet of the third millennium BC in Mesopotamia, there is a record of a type of sausage. Because making sausages means that no part of the animal goes to waste, it is unsurprising that the sausage is made and eaten worldwide.

In England, we have many regional varieties using different herbs and spices. One of my favorites is the Lincolnshire sausage where my grandparents grew up. It is flavored with sage.

Wrapping the meat in dough has also been a practice since antiquity. However, today's sausage roll, with puff pastry encasing the moist flavorsome sausagemeat, only became recognizable in the 19th century. It became a popular street food because it is so easy to eat on the go.

I have found an early recipe for puff pastry dating from 1596 AD by Thomas Dawson. He calls it Butter Paste, and it does contain quite a quantity of butter. He describes dotting the butter on the pastry and rolling out and repeating five or six times. This is what separates the pastry into its flakey layers. Feel free to make your own, or use a bought block of puff pastry.

I have set out two variations below. One flavored with fennel seeds and the other with sage. You can tell which is which by deciding on the decoration. I used onion seeds for the sage and sesame for the fennel.

INGREDIENTS

- 1 pack (500g) ready-made puff pastry
- 1 pack of pork sausages (400g)
- ½ cup (60g) freshly-made breadcrumbs
- 1 tablespoon of fennel seeds
- 1 tablespoon chopped sage
- 1 beaten egg for the glaze
- 1 tablespoon onion seeds as decoration
- 1 tablespoon sesame seeds as decoration

METHOD

1. Preheat the oven to 400°F (200°C).
2. Roll out the pastry and divide it into two.
3. Extract the sausage meat from the sausage skins and place it in a bowl.
4. Mix in the breadcrumbs. The best way is with your hands.
5. Divide the mixture in two.
6. To one half, add 1 tablespoon of fennel seeds, and to the other, add 1 tablespoon of chopped sage.
7. Make a long sausage shape out of each bowl of sausagemeat and place them on each half of the pastry.
8. Roll each up, sealing along the edge with the beaten egg.
9. Brush the tops of the long roll with the beaten egg.
10. Sprinkle one with onion seeds and the other with sesame seeds.

11. Chop into bite-size pieces and transfer to a baking sheet.

12. Bake in the oven for 25 minutes until cooked through and golden brown.

These are so welcome at teatime and provide a delicious foil to the sweetness of the treats to come.

17. MINI QUICHES

INTRODUCTION

The quiche is such a versatile teatime treat. It has a shortcrust pastry base and a savory egg custard filling. I think my favorite is Quiche Lorraine, which uses bacon and cheese and smoked salmon and dill quiches.

FUN FACTS

Originating in Medieval Germany, Lorraine, when France conquered that part of Germany, the recipe gained popularity.

The word quiche is from the German *Kuchen*, meaning cake. Originally it consisted of eggs, cream, and bacon, with the addition of cheese coming later.

The English have enjoyed using eggs and cream in a pastry case since at least the 14th century. However, the first mention of Quiche Lorraine was sometime after World War II, when British soldiers brought the recipe home. There are now endless variations to Quiche Lorraine, and I've included a smoked salmon and dill quiche that I love to make.

INGREDIENTS FOR QUICHE LORRAINE

Serves 24

- 13.2oz. (375g) shortcrust pastry
- 6 rashers of bacon
- 3 eggs
- ¾ cup (180ml) heavy (double) cream
- ½ cup (100g) grated cheese
- Pinch of salt and pepper to taste

METHOD

1. Preheat the oven to 350°F (180°C). Grease and flour your little pie pans.
2. Unroll your ready-rolled pastry or roll it out on a lightly floured surface. Cut out 24 circles using a 3¼-inch or 8cm round pastry cutter. You should be able to get 24. You will need to gather it up and roll it out again, though.
3. Use the circles to line the pie tins. There is no need to bake blind.
4. Chop the bacon into pieces and fry until golden in a frying pan with a tablespoon of oil.
5. Pop a few pieces of bacon in each pastry case.
6. Mix the eggs, cream, salt, and pepper in a jug.
7. Pour the creamy mixture over the bacon and sprinkle a little cheese on top.
8. Bake in the oven for 20 minutes until golden brown.

FOR THE SMOKED SALMON AND DILL QUICHES:

Replace the bacon and cheese with ½ cup (100g) chopped smoked salmon and 1 tablespoon of chopped dill. Scatter some of the smoked salmon in each pastry case. Add the tablespoon of fresh dill to the cream mixture before pouring into each pastry case. Continue to bake as above.

Delicious served at teatime as a savory before the sweet teatime treats are consumed.

18. CHEESE AND ONION SQUARE TARTS

INTRODUCTION

This uses puff pastry which adds a lightness to the caramelized onion and cream filling. Also, it's a rather welcome change to have a square tart rather than the usual round ones.

FUN FACTS

Studies have revealed that cheese and onion is the British people's favorite flavor - from crisps to pies. Cheddar cheese has been made on these shores since the 12th century, originally by a monk in the village of Cheddar in Somerset.

Since Joseph Harding invented cheddaring in 1857, this process has been used to create Cheddar. It was a revolutionary process that suppressed the growth of microorganisms that caused bacteria. The process involves stacking pieces of curd on top of one another and pressing to remove the whey. The cheese is then aged. Mature Cheddar is left to mature for at least nine months.

I suggest using a mature cheddar in this recipe as it contrasts so well with the sweetness of the caramelized onions.

Incidentally, there is a recorded recipe for onion tart from 1390 AD from the Master Cooks of King Richard II, which also uses onions, butter, and cream, with the addition of saffron and raisins. So we're in good ancient company with this recipe.

INGREDIENTS

Makes 12 individual tarts

- 13.2oz. (375g) ready-rolled puff pastry
- 2 medium-sized onions (about 400g)- sliced
- ¼ cup or ½ stick (60g) butter
- 2 eggs
- ½ cup (120ml) heavy (double) cream
- 1 tablespoon chopped sage or thyme
- 2 tablespoon grated cheese - preferable a sharp or mature Cheddar cheese or similar
- Salt and pepper

METHOD

1. Preheat the oven to 400°F (200°C).
2. Unroll your puff pastry and divide it into 12 roughly equal squares. I find it easiest to cut the pastry into three long strips and then cut each strip into quarters. This gives you 12 squares.
3. Place each square onto a baking sheet. Score a thin border of a few millimeters inside each square which will form the edge of each tart when cooked, and place in the oven for 10 minutes.
4. While the pastry is cooking, gently heat the butter and the onions so the onions turn a pale golden and are caramelized - it will take about 15-20 minutes, but it is well worth the time as crunchy onion in a tart is best avoided.
5. Remove the pastry from the oven, and you should have 12 squares of pastry, each puffed up. Push down the inner square with your finger, leaving the puffed-up edge.
6. Divide the onions into 12 and place a twelfth in the middle of each pastry tart.
7. Mix the eggs, cream, and sage or thyme, and season with salt and pepper.

8. Spoon over one tablespoon of the creamy mixture onto each tart and finish with a teaspoon of grated cheese.

9. Bake in the oven for a further 15 minutes until nicely golden and set.

These little tarts are delicious as a savory part of teatime and a welcome change from the sandwich.

MINI-PUDS

19. MINI-KNICKERBOCKER GLORY

INTRODUCTION

This is such an iconic dish. It is traditionally served in a conical glass. It consists of ice cream layered with fruit and syrups and cream, topped off with a cherry. These stripes of red raspberry syrup and white ice cream make it look like the old-fashioned knickerbockers.

FUN FACTS

An early version originated in New York in the early 1900s. The Knickerbocker Hotel in Manhattan, New York, was pink and cream, and when it was closed down in the early 1900s, a pink and cream dish was created in its honor. At some point, it made the transatlantic crossing and became wildly popular in England.

I remember having these as a child, and they were topped with sprinkles, which provided a bit of a bite along with the sweetness.

These Mini-Knickerbocker Glories can form the showstopper of your teatime selection.

There are limitless variations of this dish, but to be authentic, it must maintain the red and white stripes, or it is just an ice cream sundae. So use your imagination between the red and white layers. Anything goes!

I suggest making a delicious fresh raspberry sauce or coulis, but you can use an ice cream syrup if you prefer.

INGREDIENTS

Makes 8

- Vanilla ice cream - 16 small scoops
- 1¼ cups (200g) raspberries
- 1 tin (410g) sliced peaches in juice, chopped into small chunks
- 1 cup (240ml) heavy (double) cream, whipped into soft peaks, or a can of aerosol cream
- 8 raspberries to garnish

For the raspberry coulis:

- 1½ cups (250g) raspberries
- 2 tablespoons powdered (icing) sugar

METHOD

1. Make the raspberry coulis by heating the raspberries with the sugar and a tablespoon of water until the sugar has dissolved. Mash the raspberries and pass them through a sieve to get rid of the seeds and retain the juices.
2. Set yourself up with the coulis, a dish of raspberries, peaches, whipped cream, ice cream, and the pots you're using to serve.
3. Place about 4 chunks of peach and 2 or 3 raspberries, depending on their size, in the bottom of each pot. Add a tablespoon of coulis.
4. Add a small scoop of ice cream. I flatten the ice cream so that it sits as a layer in the pot.
5. Add another layer of fruit and coulis as before, followed by a layer of ice cream.
6. Finally, top with a blob of cream and raspberry to garnish.
7. Drizzle over about a tablespoon of coulis to finish.

Serve immediately with a teaspoon, and enjoy!

20. CHOCOLATE MOUSSE

INTRODUCTION

No recipe book that includes desserts or mini-puds is complete without a recipe for chocolate mousse. This one is rich and very satisfying. It's made with just three ingredients: chocolate, sugar, and eggs.

FUN FACTS

Mousse is a French word that means foam. It is the foam derived from whipping the egg whites into soft peaks until airy that gives it the desired effect. Once the Spanish had introduced chocolate to the rest of Europe, it was only a matter of time before cooking with chocolate and creating a chocolate mousse emerged.

Egg yolks are often stirred into the melted chocolate as it creates a richer feel. Chilling the mousse makes the texture a little denser and more satisfying.

I would encourage you to use the best chocolate you can find, as your mousse will taste so much better with a higher cocoa solids percentage.

You may be wondering why it's necessary to whip the sugar into the egg whites rather than just adding it to the yolks. This is so that the sugar can dissolve. Otherwise, you get a rather unattractive sand-like crunch to your smooth chocolate mousse. I can tell you this through experimenting with this myself!

INGREDIENTS

Makes 8 depending on your pot size.

- 1¼ cups (200g) 70% dark chocolate, plus an extra piece to grate over to serve
- 3 large or 4 medium eggs, separated
- 3 tablespoon superfine (caster) sugar

METHOD

1. Melt the chocolate in a bowl over simmering water or in the microwave stirring every 30 seconds, until just melted, and set aside.
2. Whisk the egg whites to soft peaks.
3. Add the sugar and whisk again until the mixture forms stiff peaks.
4. Mix the egg yolks in with the chocolate.
5. Loosen the chocolate mixture with a heaped tablespoon of the egg whites and sugar mixture.
6. Then fold in the remaining egg whites and sugar mixture into the chocolate and yolks.
7. Carefully spoon into the mini pots and leave them to set in the fridge for 2-3 hours.
8. Decorate with grated chocolate.

Serve with a teaspoon to enjoy straight from the pots.

21. JUNKET

INTRODUCTION

Don't let the name put you off - I think it's time for Junket to make a comeback. Historic, nutritious, and delicious!

Junket is made by setting milk with rennet. Although that may not sound very appetizing - I wouldn't include this little gem unless it delivered so much more than the ingredients and name suggest. Give it a go, and I can guarantee you will become a Junket fan!

FUN FACTS

In Medieval England, Junket was made with cream for the nobility and was flavored with rosewater and spices. I have recreated that recipe here. Rum also was used to flavor the curds. If you fancy, you can substitute the rosewater for ½ teaspoon of vanilla extract.

It is traditionally served with soft fruit, but I have added an attractive layer of raspberries at the bottom, making the puds look very pretty.

It has great health-giving properties and used to be served to patients in hospitals to aid convalescence because it is nutritious and easily digested.

Rennet can be purchased in a health food shop or online. I am using vegetarian rennet. The quantity needed varies depending on the type you buy, so do check on the bottle.

INGREDIENTS

Makes 10

- 2½ cups (600ml) full-fat milk
- 2 tablespoons superfine (caster) sugar
- 1 teaspoon rosewater
- 1 teaspoon rennet - but check your rennet bottle for the exact amount
- Grated nutmeg to serve

The layer of raspberries:

- 4 tablespoons raspberries
- 1 tablespoon superfine (caster) sugar

METHOD

1. Dissolve the sugar with the raspberries in a small pan.
2. Place a teaspoon of this mixture in the bottom of your pots, being careful that you don't smear the sides of the pots, and set to one side.
3. Heat the milk so that it's warm, not more than blood temperature.
4. Whisk in the sugar and the rosewater.
5. Add the rennet and stir through. You need to act fairly quickly once the rennet is added because it will begin to set.
6. Pour so the Junket travels down the inside of the pot so as not to disturb the raspberry layer.
7. Let the puddings cool to room temperature and then set in the fridge for 1-2 hours.
8. Generously grate nutmeg over the top before serving.

Enjoy as the Medieval nobility did!

22. MINI-FRUIT CHEESECAKES

INTRODUCTION

No baking is required for these cheesecakes. They are creamy and sweet above a buttery biscuit base.

FUN FACTS

It is thought that a rudimentary form of cheesecake was first made in ancient Greece using patties of curd cheese mixed with honey and flour before being baked.

There is a recipe for Roman *Savillum* or cheesecake dating from the second century BC, which used four ingredients, cheese, honey, egg, and flour. It doesn't have the pastry base, though.

The pastry base was added during the late medieval ages in Europe. The first known English cookbook, written in 1390 AD by the chef to Richard II, included an elderflower cheesecake recipe called *Sambocade*, after the Latin word for elderflower. Over the next six centuries, the English have devised many variations to this delicious idea of combining creamy cheese and sugar and fruits.

Unsurprisingly, the cheesecake made its way to America, where it has been very popular ever since.

For mini-cheesecakes, I used a special tin that has mini loose-bottomed bases so the cheesecakes can be released easily. However, you can use muffin cases instead and just release the cheesecakes from the cases when ready to serve. Another option is to use a little 2oz. pot and leave the cheesecake in the pot for the eater to enjoy using a teaspoon.

INGREDIENTS

Makes 24

- ¼ cup or ½ stick (60g) butter, melted
- 9 Graham crackers or 9 digestive biscuits (140g) crushed
- 1½ cups (340g) cream cheese
- ½ cup (100g) superfine (caster) sugar
- ¾ cup (180ml) heavy (double) cream
- Zest and juice of 1 lemon
- Fruit to decorate, strawberries and raspberries

METHOD

1. Melt the butter and mix in the Graham crackers or digestive biscuits.
2. Press a level tablespoon of this biscuit base firmly into the bottom of each of your cheesecake pots and leave to cool in the fridge while you make the filling.
3. Whisk together the cream cheese, sugar, cream, lemon zest, and juice until thick.
4. Spoon the creamy mixture into the cheesecake molds or pots.
5. Decorate with the fruit of your choice.
6. Leave to solidify in the fridge for a few hours before you release the cheesecakes from their molds and serve. Or until you serve them in their little pots.

23. SYLLABUB

INTRODUCTION

This is a mini-pud that mixes heavy (double) cream with sugar and wine. The ingredients combine beautifully to make a light fragrant treat.

FUN FACTS

The word syllabub comes from the name *Sille*, from the Champagne region of France, and the word *bub*, which was an Elizabethan slang word meaning a bubbling drink. Hence *Sille bub* – wine mixed with a frothy cream.

This dates back to the 17th century when milk was used instead of cream and purportedly was directed straight from the cow's udder into a bowl of sweetened cider sack, a bit like sherry. This gave a natural froth to the dish. It was left to curdle and then drunk.

It seems, however, that the preparation of this dish is likely to have been a little more involved in order to produce something delicious and not just a stringy lump of curds above an alcoholic whey!

The foamy part later became the main interest and now forms the only element in the pudding. As I have here, a more solid version involves cream and wine. It is a cream whip rather than a drink. I can assure you there will be no stringy curds, just delicious velvety cream!

INGREDIENTS

Makes 10

- 1 cup (240ml) heavy (double) cream
- ½ cup (100g) superfine (caster) sugar
- ¼ cup (60ml) sweet white wine (or apple juice)
- Zest and juice of 1 lemon
- Mint leaves for garnish

METHOD

1. Whip the cream with the sugar.
2. Whip in the wine, lemon juice, and zest.
3. Pile into your dishes and garnish with a mint leaf.
4. Chill in the fridge until you are ready to serve.

24. ETON MESS

INTRODUCTION

This mini-pud consists of crushed meringues, cream, and strawberries. It evokes a wonderful feeling of summer.

FUN FACTS

Eton Mess was first mentioned in print in 1893 and is a dessert made with whipped cream, meringues, and strawberries. The story goes that a pudding of meringue, cream, and strawberries was served at the annual cricket match between two exclusive English public schools, Eton College and Harrow School. The pudding was dropped, scraped off the floor, and served under its new name, "Eton Mess." It is still served at the annual cricket match between the schools to this day.

A similar dessert is served year-round at Lancing College, West Sussex, made with bananas instead of strawberries. So if you fancy, do try substituting bananas for strawberries.

Small wild strawberries have been enjoyed in England since time immemorial and still grow wild. Modern strawberries were imported from the U.S. in the 16th century and are the larger juicier ones. Feel free to hunt for wild strawberries, grow them, or buy them.

INGREDIENTS

Makes 10

- 2 cups (480ml) whipping cream or double cream
- 4½ cups (600g) strawberries
- 1 tablespoon superfine (caster) sugar
- 4 cups (110g) or 1 packet of 8 ready-made meringue nests

METHOD

1. Cut the strawberries into eighths and sprinkle over the superfine (caster) sugar and leave to macerate.
2. Break the meringues into ½ inch (1 cm) pieces and place them in a bowl.
3. Whip the cream to the floppy stage. Don't overwhip because you want it to be soft and velvety. This can all be done in advance.
4. When you are ready to eat the pudding, fold together the meringues, cream, strawberries, and juices, saving 9 strawberry pieces for decoration.

Decorate and serve immediately with a teaspoon.

25. LEMON POSSET AND SHORTBREAD BUTTONS

LEMON POSSET

INTRODUCTION

I have used disposable shot glasses for these possets. You can either serve them alone or accompanied with shortbread buttons. I have included a recipe for these buttons below.

FUN FACTS

Posset used to mean a medieval warm drink; as Shakespeare wrote for Lady Macbeth, "*I have drugg'd their possets.*" In the 16th century, it first became known as the delicious dessert that we would recognize. I always get so much pleasure from thinking that I am eating something that my ancestors must have enjoyed 500 years ago - assuming they could afford the sugar, of course!

There is a wonderful story that the posset was such a popular dessert that when Queen Mary of England became betrothed to Prince Phillip II of Spain in 1554, the Spanish Ambassador gave them a posset set made from crystal, gold, precious gems, and enamel. The story goes that it was on display at Hatfield House in Hertfordshire. I was so delighted with this story that I began preparing to visit Hatfield House to see the set for myself.

However, I received a phone call from the former Head of Collections informing me that this was just a fable, probably started in the Victorian era. The crystal items on display were not from a posset set as they are far too valuable to have been used in cooking and were not given to Queen Mary on her betrothal. I am indebted to Robin Harcourt Williams, former Head of Collections of Hatfield House, for this clarification. I can see how the story persisted as it is a wonderfully romantic notion.

Although the story turned out to be a disappointment, this pudding will not!

INGREDIENTS

Makes 10

- 2 cups (480ml) heavy (double) cream
- 1 cup (200g) superfine (caster) sugar
- Zest and juice of 2 lemons

METHOD

1. Heat the cream, sugar, and lemon zest in a large pan and bring to a gentle simmer.
2. Simmer for about 3 minutes.
3. Turn off the heat and add the lemon juice and stir thoroughly. It will thicken a little.
4. Pour out the posset into your chosen containers and place in the fridge to set (about 3 hours).
5. Serve sprinkled with powdered sugar with a little spoon.
6. You may wish to serve these with shortbread buttons. I included a recipe for shortbread in my first book, *English Teatime Treats: Delicious Traditional Recipes Made Simple*, but I have set it out here using half the quantity of the ingredients which provides two buttons per mini-pud. They work very well together.

SHORTBREAD BUTTONS

INGREDIENTS

Makes about 20 shortbread buttons

- ½ cup or 1 stick (110g) butter
- ½ teaspoon vanilla extract
- ½ cup (65g) powdered (icing) sugar

- ½ cup (60g) cornstarch (cornflour)
- ¾ cups (100g) all-purpose (plain) flour
- Superfine (caster) sugar to sprinkle.

METHOD

1. Preheat the oven to 350°F (180°C).
2. Place the butter in a pan and warm through so the butter is almost melted.
3. Remove from the heat and add the vanilla extract.
4. Put the pan to one side while you prepare your cookie sheet. Place a sheet of parchment paper over the cookie sheet. There is no need to butter it since there's plenty of butter in the mixture.
5. Add the powdered sugar, cornstarch (cornflour), and flour to the pan and mix gently. You do not want to handle this too much, or else the texture will be too doughy.
6. Take a scant teaspoon of the mixture, form it into a little ball and press down on the parchment paper with your thumb to create the button.
7. Bake in the oven for about 10 minutes. They should be a pale golden brown when cooked.
8. Sprinkle with superfine (caster) sugar and leave to cool on the cookie sheets because they are quite fragile until cool.

Serve your lemon possets with shortbread buttons and a little teaspoon.

26. FLUMMERY

INTRODUCTION

What a wonderful name for a pudding! This is made with gelatin and evaporated milk which forms a jelly or Jell-O in the U.S. I've added decorative cream on top. For such simple ingredients, it is surprisingly tasty and almost melts in the mouth.

FUN FACTS

Unlike the jams or fruit spreads in America, Jellies are gelatin-set fruit desserts that can take elaborate forms. Jellies have been recorded from as early as 1520 AD, when Henry VIII had jelly at his Garter feast.

Having recently visited Hampton Court Palace, where Henry VIII lived, I had a wonderful tour of his kitchens. To create the amazing feasts he enjoyed, the kitchens would have made quite cramped cooking conditions. An encouragement to us all to bake no matter how small our kitchens are!

This idea of setting jelly as a dessert became more and more popular. In his cookbook from 1660 AD, Robert May suggested molding jellies in scallop shells and other kinds of seashells which is very inventive.

The Victorians used different shaped molds for their desserts. They used calves foot jelly prepared by boiling calves' feet overnight and using the liquid to set the jelly, which was flavored with lemons, cinnamon, and sugar. The delights served after all the savory courses were supposed to have some sort of comic element involved, and wobbling jellies hit the spot for the Victorians.

Flummery is a type of jelly made with cream or milk, so it is opaque. It was traditionally made with oatmeal that was left for 48 hours and drained. It was that liquid that then set the flummery.

Hannah Glasse sets out a recipe in her book dated from 1747 AD, which uses hartshorn to set the flummery. These are shavings of antlers. I can't imagine how this was discovered as a setting agent!

Living by the sea, I have tried using seaweed as a setting agent - which works very well - except for the slightly salty flavor.

Flummery became popular as an easy dessert in post-war Britain. It has waned in its popularity recently, and I think it could do with a renaissance.

INGREDIENTS

Makes 12, 2oz. pots

- 85g pack of Jell-O (or 1 block of 135g jelly) with 1 cup (240ml) boiling water
- 12 fl oz. (350g) evaporated milk
- Aerosol cream to decorate

METHOD

1. Mix the Jell-O or jelly with the boiling water and stir until dissolved.
2. Stir in the evaporated milk.
3. Carefully pour into your pots and leave to set overnight.
4. Decorate with a squirt of cream and serve with a little spoon as part of your teatime spread.

27. SUMMER PUDDINGS

INTRODUCTION

These are summer fruit puddings made with bread, sugar, and summer fruits. Left to set for a few hours, it allows all the flavors to meld and the bread to soften to allow you to taste summer.

FUN FACTS

A recipe for Summer Pudding was first published in 1895. But I can't help but think it was made before then, as the ingredients would have been easily available to peasants and nobility alike.

A recipe uses cherries and sugar and is thickened with breadcrumbs from the Medieval book from 1390 AD, *The Forme of Cury*. Perhaps this was the inspiration for what we know as Summer Pudding.

I have layered the bread so that it is visible through the outside of the clear pot. You may be thinking that the bread may not work very well with the fruit, but I can assure you it is transformed by the sugar and fruits to become unrecognizable as bread - just a delicious soft sweet fruitiness.

Traditionally, this is turned out and eaten as a dessert. However, at teatime, I don't think that is very practical. I have created mini-puds that can easily be eaten straight from the pot just with a teaspoon.

INGREDIENTS

Makes 4

- 2½-3 cups (400g), depending on how densely packed your fruit is, mixed berries, fresh or frozen (I used raspberries, blackberries, redcurrants, blueberries, and strawberries)
- 4 tablespoons superfine (caster) sugar
- Zest 1 lemon
- 3-4 slices slightly stale white bread, crusts removed
- Aerosol cream or whipped cream

METHOD

1. Reserve 4 small berries for decoration and put all the rest, apart from the strawberries, into a pan and sprinkle over the sugar.

2. Put the pan over low heat until the sugar has dissolved and the fruit has started to release its juices.

3. Increase the heat, bring the mixture to a boil, then simmer for 3 minutes until the fruit is soft and there are lots of deep red juices.

4. Quarter the strawberries and cut each quarter in half and stir into the berries, along with the lemon zest.

5. Remove the pan from the heat and strain the fruit through a sieve, reserving the juices.

6. Depending on the shape of your pots, use the pot to cut out 4 squares for the top of the pudding and 4 smaller squares for the middle of the pot.

7. Set yourself up with your pots, the juice in a bowl, and the fruit in a separate bowl. I find it easier to make all 4 puddings simultaneously so that you can more easily judge the quantities.

8. Carefully add a tablespoon of the strained fruit into the bottom of the pots and add some juice to cover.

9. Dip the smaller squares of bread into the reserved juices and place them over the fruit in each pot. Press lightly in place, trying to avoid creating air bubbles.

10. Add another layer of fruit and juice and top off with the larger square of bread dipped in juice.

11. Cover the top of the pots with cling film and push down firmly with your fingers. Pop in the fridge to chill for at least 4 hrs, preferably overnight.

Decorate with a squirt of aerosol cream or dollop of whipped cream topped with a reserved berry and serve with a small spoon.

28. FOOLS

INTRODUCTION

You can make a fool out of any fruit. I have used strawberries, but any seasonal fruit that you have or fancy will work well.

FUN FACTS

First recorded in the time of Charles II, in *The Complete Cook*, the cook wrote down a recipe for gooseberry fool.

The name fool probably came from the French word *fouler*, which means to mash. So it is reasonable to suggest that some kind of mashed fruit was there from the beginning.

Traditionally, it is made by folding stewed fruit into custard. Modern recipes use whipped cream, which is what I have used. There are plenty of other desserts that use custard, and this works beautifully with cream creating a fresh fruity lightness to the recipe. There is no need to stew the strawberries.

INGREDIENTS

Makes 10

- 3 cups (454g) strawberries
- 1 cup (240ml) heavy (double) cream
- ½ cup (70g) superfine (caster) sugar

METHOD

1. Puree most of the strawberries and sugar together, reserving a few for decoration.
2. Whip the cream so that it forms soft peaks.
3. Fold through the pureed fruit so it appears in streaks.
4. Carefully spoon in the fool to your serving pots.

Decorate with the reserved fruit and serve with a small spoon.

29. TRIFLE

INTRODUCTION

This is a chilled dish of three layers. The essential ingredients are sponge cake soaked in sherry or white wine with fruit or jam, custard, and whipped cream. It is usually served in a large clear bowl to show off the layers. I have used 4oz. clear serving pots as it is so pretty to see the layers.

FUN FACTS

The name comes from the custom of giving end-of-meal sweetmeats some sort of slightly comic title to indicate an unimportant or trivial thing, as is the probable derivation of flan, meaning to trifle and fool.

In the 16th century, trifle was made with thick cream, sugar, ginger, and rosewater. It developed from the fool, and the two names originally were interchangeable. When jelly was added in the 18th century, the trifle began a life of its own.

In England, many people make and serve a trifle at Christmas as part of their family tradition. These mini-trifles could be incorporated into the Christmas teatime feast along with the Christmas cake.

I have not added jelly in the recipe below as I feel the texture and taste are better without it. Although there are three layers to prepare, please don't be put off as it is very quick and straightforward. It gives you more time to make other teatime treats! You can buy really good ready-made custards, especially those available fresh in tubs.

INGREDIENTS

Makes 10 mini-trifles using 10, 4oz. pots

For the custard

Either use a tub of ready-made custard or make your own:

- 2 tablespoons of instant custard powder such as Birds Custard Powder
- 2 tablespoons superfine (caster) sugar
- 2½ cups (1 pint or 568ml) full-fat milk

For the fruit and cake base

- 1 small pound cake or Madeira cake
- 10 tablespoons of sherry or orange juice
- 2 cups (320g) frozen mixed berries

For the cream topping

- 1 cup (240ml) heavy (double) cream, whipped
- ¼ cup (30g) powdered (icing) sugar
- Sprinkles to decorate

METHOD

For the custard

1. Mix 2 tablespoons of custard powder with 2 tablespoons of superfine (caster) sugar and a little milk to form a paste.
2. Heat the remaining milk and whisk in the custard powder mixture.
3. Heat until thickened. Set aside to cool.

For the fruit and cake base

1. Slice your pound cake or Madeira cake and cut squares or circles to fit into the base of your serving pots.

2. Pour over 1 tablespoon of orange juice or sherry.

3. Add a tablespoon of mixed berries.

For the cream topping

1. Softly whip the cream, add the powdered (icing) sugar, and set to one side.

Putting it all together

1. Carefully add about a tablespoon of the cooled custard as the next layer on top of the berries in each pot.

2. Finish off with a tablespoon of whipped cream and decorate with sprinkles.

Leave in the fridge to chill, which will allow the flavors to develop and mix. Serve with a little spoon to be eaten straight from the pots.

30. APPLE SNOW

INTRODUCTION

Don't let the simplicity of these ingredients let you imagine it tastes dull. It has become a firm favorite in my house, and the combination of the sharp apples, sweet creaminess of the snow, and the lightness of the lemons work to perfection.

FUN FACTS

Although we may think of Apple Snow as a simple dish to prepare, it first appeared as an extravagant end to a feast.

In the 16th century, egg whites were beaten with a whisk of birch twigs to produce an attractive foam. This foam was then beaten with thick cream, rosewater, and sugar. It was then built up over an apple and spread on the twigs of a rosemary branch to look like real snow. In some versions, the snow was gilded as a final touch. This Elizabethan dishful of snow, as it was called, was a spectacular centerpiece for the banquet course following a festal meal.

In the 18th century, whipped apple pulp was added and came to be known as Apple Snow. This was eaten cold.

INGREDIENTS

Makes 10

- About 2 (or 500g) medium Bramley apples or another sharp-tasting apple like Granny Smith (about 4 of these smaller apples), peeled and finely chopped
- ½ cup (100g) superfine (caster) sugar
- Zest and juice of 1 lemon
- 1 egg white
- ½ cup (120ml) heavy (double) cream

METHOD

1. Place the chopped apple, lemon zest and juice, and most of the sugar (reserving 3 tablespoons for later) in a pan. Cover and simmer for 15 minutes until the apple has broken down.
2. If the apple hasn't broken down enough, whizz the mixture until it is pureed.
3. Meanwhile, whisk the egg whites until they form soft peaks, and add the remaining 3 tablespoons of sugar one at a time to the whipped egg whites.
4. Fold the whisked egg mixture into the apples.
5. Whip the cream until it has soft peaks and fold it through the apple and egg white mixture.
6. Carefully spoon into your serving pots and pop into the fridge until you are ready to serve them.

I have decorated the apple snow with elderflower blossom, but use whatever edible flowers are available for a pretty topping. I do think this is particularly delicious served with a buttery crunch of Shortbread Buttons (see Lemon Posset and Shortbread Buttons recipe).

APPENDIX – PASTRY TIPS

INTRODUCTION

Don't let requiring a pastry base put you off! If you don't fancy making your pastry, you don't have to! There are some terrific ready-made pastries available and even ready-cooked pastry shells.

Ready-Made Pastry - be guilt-free!

I like to think of it as having my own sous-chef giving me a helping hand! And what great chef doesn't have a sous-chef to help with the more basic and time-consuming tasks?

You have two options, either buy the tart shells ready-baked and good to go, or buy a ready-made pastry, either in a block or ready-rolled and use that to line your tarts. Let's look at both options.

Ready-baked pastry cases

All you do is to make one of the fillings yourself. Using a ready-baked pastry shell is such a quick way to produce a delicious tart.

I encourage you to try to buy pastry cases that are made with butter as the flavor will be much better. You can buy the small tartlet shells or the larger tarts.

Ready-made pastry, either in a block or ready-rolled

If you fancy being a little more hands-on with the pastry, you can buy a block of ready-made pastry or a pack of ready-rolled pastry. The advantage is that it is already rested and will not shrink when you cook it.

Puff pastry, however, takes much longer to make, and I would recommend buying it ready-made. The results with ready-made puff pastry are so good that it doesn't seem worth your time and energy to make it from scratch.

If you are not in a hurry, have a go at making your own pastry. It is straightforward and delicious!

MAKE YOUR OWN PASTRY

There seems to have grown up a great mystery about pastry-making, and it is sometimes perceived as a complicated and challenging art. But, with a few pointers in mind, it doesn't take long and is very straightforward.

It is impressive that you haven't skipped over this section and moved straight back to the recipes!

You can make it by hand or use a food processor. The advantage of the processor is that it keeps all the ingredients cool, but it is easy to over-work the pastry. If you don't mind a bit of extra washing up, then use the food processor. But if you like to get your hands into the mixture - and it is rather therapeutic - then have a go with your fingertips.

TOP TIPS FOR FANTASTIC PASTRY EVERY TIME

1. Keep everything cool - including yourself!
2. Always rub in the fat into the flour before adding any other ingredients.
3. Make sure the fat is well rubbed in - like breadcrumbs.
4. Only add cold liquids.
5. Allow the pastry to rest before using it for at least 30 minutes.
6. Always use a preheated oven.
7. Always place your cake pan onto a preheated baking sheet as this will keep the bottom crisp as no one likes a soggy bottom!

SHORTCRUST PASTRY

You need all-purpose (plain) flour, butter, salt, and cold water. The usual adage is "half fat to flour," but that is by weight, so only works if you are working in grams. If you are using cup measurements, I have set out the volumes you need.

Shortcrust pastry can be used for everything, but if you like your pastry a little sweeter, I have set out a sweet pastry recipe as well.

RECIPE FOR SHORTCRUST PASTRY

Ingredients

This makes 12 oz. (375g) shortcrust pastry enough to line a 9 inch (23 cm) removable bottom cake pan.

- 2 cups (250g) all-purpose (plain) flour
- ½ cup (125g) butter
- 1 tsp. salt
- 2-3 tbsp. cold water as needed

This makes 18 oz. (500g) shortcrust pastry enough to line a 9 inch (23 cm) removable bottom cake pan and make the lid.

- 3 cups (375g) all-purpose (plain) flour
- ¾ cup (170g) butter
- 1½ tsp. salt
- 3-4 tbsp. cold water as needed

Method

Keep yourself and everything cool!

1. Put the flour into a bowl.
2. Add the teaspoon of salt.
3. Cut up the fat into about 1 cm cubes and coat the cubes with flour.
4. With your cool hands, rub-in the fat into the flour by lifting your hands above the bowl, which will aerate the mixture. Or if you are using a processor, gently pulse.
5. When it resembles breadcrumbs, your rubbing-in work is done.
6. Add just enough cold water, so the dough comes together into a firm ball.
7. Press the dough into a disc, sprinkle with a little flour, wrap it in cling film and pop it in the fridge for at least 30 minutes to chill.

RECIPE FOR SHORTCRUST SWEET PASTRY

Ingredients

This makes 14 oz. (425g) sweet shortcrust pastry, generous enough to line a 9 inch (23 cm) removable bottom cake pan.

- 2 cups (250g) all-purpose (plain) flour
- ½ cup (125g) butter
- ¼ cup (50g) superfine (caster) sugar
- 1 large egg
- 2 tbsp. cold milk as needed

Method

Keep yourself and everything cool!

1. Put the flour into a bowl.
2. Cut up the fat into about 1 cm cubes and coat the cubes with flour.
3. With your cool hands, rub-in the fat into the flour by lifting your hands above the bowl, which will aerate the mixture. Or if you are using a processor, gently pulse.
4. When it resembles breadcrumbs, your rubbing-in work is done.
5. Add the sugar.
6. Add the egg and enough cold milk so that the dough comes together into a firm ball.
7. Press the dough into a disc, sprinkle with a little flour, wrap it in cling film and pop it in the fridge for at least 30 minutes to chill.

HOW TO ROLL PASTRY

Whether you have made your own pastry or bought a ready-made block, this section is for you. If you are using ready-rolled pastry, then move onto the section below, "How to Bake Blind".

1. Make a disc out of your pastry, sprinkle your cool surface with flour and place your pastry disc on top.

2. Take your rolling pin, and make indents in one direction, turn the pastry and do the same at right angles to the original indents. This will mean that the disc is about twice its original size.

3. Roll out the pastry from the middle away from you, in three short bursts. Turn the pastry 90 degrees and repeat until the dough is the right size for your cake pan.

HOW TO LINE YOUR CAKE PAN

Once you have rolled out your pastry or unrolled your ready-rolled pastry, it is time to line your cake pan.

I think it is best to use a metal pan with a removable bottom so that the tart will come out much easier. If you are using a non-stick pan, then please grease it before sprinkling it with a little flour. There is nothing more upsetting than being unable to get your beautiful creation out of its pan!

1. Ensure the pastry is the right size by carefully placing the cake pan on top of your rolled-out pastry and judging whether there is enough pastry to go up the sides.

2. Take your rolling pin and place the pastry half over the rolling pin and move it over your cake pan.

3. Gently drop the pastry over your tin. Lift the edges to allow the pastry to fall into the edges of the tin.

4. Be careful not to pull or stretch your pastry at this point; just allow it to fall.

5. Gently press it into the corners of the tin.

6. Take your rolling pin and roll over the top of the cake pan. This will sever the excess pastry from your lined tin.

7. Slightly loosen the edges of the pastry with your fingers so that the top is not stuck to the rim.

HOW TO BAKE BLIND

Once you have rolled out your pastry and lined your cake pan, some recipes call for the pastry to be cooked before adding the filling. This is so that the pastry is not soggy on the bottom and is nice and crispy.

1. Preheat the oven to 400°F (200°C).

2. Take some greaseproof paper, parchment paper, or lightly greased aluminum foil and place it over your pastry-lined cake pan.

3. Fill it with something that will weigh down the paper or foil, such as dried beans, or blind baking ceramic balls. Cover the base. Protect the top by ensuring the paper overlaps it so that the edges do not over-brown.

4. Place in the hot oven for 10-15 minutes.

5. Remove the paper carefully with the beans or ceramic balls and pop the cake pan back in the oven for another 10 minutes to cook the base.

6. Take out of the oven and allow to cool.

7. Your tart base is now ready to be filled!

RELEASING YOUR TART FROM THE PAN

An easy way of doing this is to stand the removable bottom cake pan on a can of beans and gently pull down the outer case, releasing your tart.

ARE ALL THESE RULES REALLY NECESSARY?

Coming from a chemistry background, I always like to know the reasons for following the exact instructions in a recipe and whether there are any corners that can successfully be cut. So, I thought it might be helpful for some explanation as to why these guidelines are suggested, and then you can make up your own mind as to whether it is worthwhile. I have suggested the following:

1. **Rest your pastry for at least 30 minutes.** If you don't, it is much softer and more difficult to handle and very likely to shrink away from the cake pan.

2. **Keep everything cold.** If the dough gets too warm, it is much more difficult to handle, and the pastry will be tougher.

3. **Add just enough water to form the dough.** If too little water is added, the pastry will be very dry and break when you try to roll it out (just add a little more water). If too much, it will be too sticky to handle (just add a little more flour).

4. **Do not overwork your pastry.** If you do, the pastry will be rather tough, which is why you need to be careful if you use a food processor.

But most importantly - enjoy and get baking!

ACKNOWLEDGEMENTS

This book would not have been possible without the amazing support from my husband and children. Thank you for all your tastings and suggestions and most importantly your encouragement!

I'm also so grateful to my editorial team at Precision Marketing to William Gaskill and his team. Thank you also to my readers for your continued support and suggestions for future books.

I love to hear from you!

ABOUT THE AUTHOR

Sandra Hawkins is qualified in many disciplines. She is a chemist, banker, lawyer, teacher, apologist, author, wife, mother of three and a qualified Indian head massage therapist! However, she also has a real passion for food and is an exceptional chef.

Combining her love for mixing things up in a chemistry lab with her natural gift as a supertaster, Sandra has always loved to experiment with cooking.

From her very first Food and Nutrition lessons at an English school (Guildford High) to exploring Indian and African cuisine while traveling and living overseas, Sandra is particularly passionate about using cooking to bring people together and to seize life's delights and transform them into moments.

This book reflects her passion for food and her unique ability to simplify complex recipes, so people can easily enjoy traditional English teatime treats at home for the first time.

Sandra is married to songwriter/producer/author, Simon Hawkins and has three beautiful children, Poppy, Monty and Barty . They live in a quiet village on a beach on the south coast of England, in West Sussex.

This is Sandra's third book on *English Teatime Treats*.

The others are:

English Teatime Treats: Delicious Traditional Recipes Made Simple

English Teatime Treats 2: The Best Recipes From Around England Made Simple

All her books are available on Amazon in print and Kindle.

www.englishteatimetreats.com

Happy Baking!

www.ingramcontent.com/pod-product-compliance
Lightning Source LLC
Chambersburg PA
CBHW061143010526
44118CB00026B/2851